Follow up
your way to
Fortune
with
Gavin Scott

**New ways to make your business click
using new technology for free**

Published by
Filament Publishing Ltd
16, Croydon Road, Waddon,
Croydon, Surrey CR0 4PA
Telephone 020 8688 2598
www.filamentpublishing.com

ISBN 978-1-905493-59-3
Printed by Advanced Book Printing, Uxbridge

Dedication

I would like to dedicate this
book to anybody trying to get
their head around using the
power of the internet
and to point them in
the right direction
to have the amazing
lifestyle that we do.

Always be open minded
to learn new things.

Enjoy!

"You can get whatever you want
in life, if you help enough other
people to get what they want"

Zig Ziglar

Contents

"The things that are easy to do,

are also easy not to do,

that's the difference

between success and failure,

pennies and fortunes"

Jim Rohn

Acknowledgements

Bonnie and I would like to thank a few people who have helped to put this book together and guided us on the path to learn the internet.

Firstly I would like to thank Lasse Rouhiainen, the video and marketing coach from Sweden, who shared some simple training that got me to see the big picture of the internet.

Secondly to Jeanette and John Hawkes for their help in shaping the book into the form it is in today.

Thanks also to Chris Day of Filament Publishing Ltd for helping to make it happen.

It is exciting for us to share this information with you. The webpage referred to regularly in the book will be updated with lots more free training.

"You become successful
the moment you start moving
towards a worthwhile goal"

PREFACE

I have written this book to share with you what has worked for us in the past and is still working for us today. I also want to introduce you to some of the new technologies which I use and which can also make a big difference to your business, making it possible for you to work smarter.

There is an old saying -
"The fortune is in the follow up"

Whatever business you are in, if you don't look after your customers somebody else will.

If you don't have any customers yet, somebody else will find them and look after them.

Technology has made building a business much easier today than it was when we first started.

Over the last 18 years we have earned literally millions using a system which still works for us to today, and which we want to share with you. However, since we first started, new technologies have come along which can really help to leverage your time. By adding them into our system, it starts to get very exciting!

But first, let me tell you my story. . . . .

"If you don't know where you are going,
you'll end up somewhere else."

MY STORY

As a child I grew up in the north-east of England. Our family went back a few generations in the ship-building industry. At school I was very poor at my studies and was put in the backward class for English. I only found out that I was dyslexic after I left school.

In the final year at High School I did a week of work experience at Newcastle Weather Centre. However, A-Levels were needed for the job and getting A-Level English looked impossible with myself being dyslexic. We had a lesson on careers every week in which we had to find a job for life.

However, I had no idea what I wanted to do.

I followed my Dad into the shipyard and
started training as a fitter and turner engineer
at Swan Hunter.

One day I overheard one of the class who had a friend who had left school, was making a fortune and he was rubbish at school.

This gave me my first hope.

If somebody else was earning a fortune, so could I.

One day, just after I left school, my Nana was betting on the football pools lottery. I put on a small amount and said I wanted to win, so I didn't have to work. My Nana laughed. She said you will have to get a job and work for the rest of your life.

My mind was made up. I had to find a hobby which would also be my job. I was not going to work all my life in a job.

However, where do you start? In those days you were told, just get a trade and you are set for life. So I followed my Dad into the shipyard and started training as a fitter and turner engineer at Swan Hunter. At that time 40,000 people worked in the shipyards.

The first year's training was at a training centre and the subsequent four years were on the ships, and maintenance in the shipyard. I remember climbing a crane in a snowstorm with no safety equipment. I could have fallen and died and all for £30 per week!

At 18 I took up surfing, and was the worst at it!
However I would not quit. I saw other people doing it
and I thought if they can so can I!

My heart was never in the shipyard. I started playing football at weekends and at 17 ended up being captain of a team of people up to the age of 30.

I was asked five times to be Best Man, but made the excuse I could not do it, but really I was frightened to make the speech.

How that has changed now. Sometimes I am speaking in front of 7,000 people. I'll tell you how that changed later.

At 18 I took up surfing, and was the worst at it. However I would not quit. It took over half my life. I saw other people doing it and I thought if they can so can I!

Every penny I earned in the shipyard went on surfing trips around the UK and Europe. At the age of 26 I won my first local competition. I was starting to get sick of working in the shipyard and wanted to spend more time surfing. The shipyard had only been a stop gap job and yet ten years on, I was still there. Are you the same?

So, I started looking at ways my hobby could be my job.

I started making surfboards. It was messy and there was not much money in it.

"You don't see anybody driving to the
shipyard in a Porsche"

However the wet suit I was using was made by a man in Devon and he was driving around in a Porsche 911.

I thought, well you don't see anybody driving to the shipyard in a Porsche. So once again I said, if he can do it so can I. All my friends told me it would not work. Why do people always try to knock you?

Well, I would prove them wrong.

I spent £2,000 on a special sewing machine and then a lot of money on rubber. I then went to night classes to learn pattern drafting. So there I was with twenty women, learning how to make frocks, etc and boy did they take the Mickey out of me.

However, if you want to be good at anything, you have to learn.

Soon I was earning more part-time by making two wet suits a week, than I was earning full-time. This went on for a few years and it was getting to the stage that I had to leave the shipyard and go full-time.

However, jobs in the shipyard were going down from 40,000 when I started, to 6,000 when I left. What was worrying me was the cost of going full-time. I knew from the shipyard that it was just a job and people don't work very hard for a boss.

Also, they stole as much as they could. Added to this was rent and rates of a factory unit, etc.

Just when I was about to go full-time, I saw a friend with a badge and asked what the silly badge was. A few days later I popped round to find out why they were so excited. I was shown a video and I saw the circles.

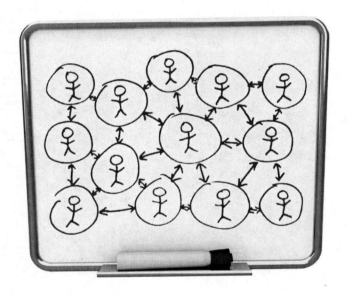

If you found six people, who just found four people and they just found two.

I was so excited about those circles I could not sleep for six weeks. I was filling every circle myself with people I knew, never mind other people finding other people. So whilst in the shipyard I was drawing circles on the sides of the ships and expecting everybody to join. However, you have to understand that not everybody will see what you can see.

The Power of Belief

When we started out in the business some 18 years ago, we knew that if somebody else could make it work, then so could we.

At the time, the company we were looking at was already some 70 years old and it had a great track record. We were further convinced that joining was the right thing to do because of the stories we were told about other people who had joined over the years and had either made a good living or even a fortune.

Stories are very powerful when sharing the opportunity with other people as they provide proof that it works and also help to give people confidence that they too can succeed.

In 1954, nobody had ever run a mile in under four minutes and it was generally believed to be impossible. In fact eminent doctors and scientists of the day worked out that the human body could not run that fast.

That was until Roger Bannister, a 25-year-old medical student in Oxford, proved them wrong and broke the record in 3 minutes 59.4 seconds. Once he achieved it, six more people did it that year and thousands have done it since. All they needed was proof that it was possible.

Roger Bannister broke the four minute mile record and proved to everyone that it was possible.

Of course, not everybody could run that fast, but it does prove a point. Once somebody has demonstrated that something can be achieved, it inspires others to set the goals to do the same - and maybe even better.

Another example of the same thing is in the highly competitive soft drinks marketplace. For years this has been dominated by two major brands, Coke and Pepsi. Both companies spend millions of pounds in advertising and promotions and you would think that the market was totally saturated.

But, for one person, all it did was give proof of what was possible, and that there was a market out there.

British entrepreneur Richard Branson confounded the experts by launching Virgin Cola and carving out a profitable section of the market for himself. I wonder how many people tried to persuade him that it couldn't be done?

As a kid you watched people driving all the time, so you know if they could, so could you.

He repeated the philosophy in the cut-throat world of aviation. Once again, a big brand dominated the marketplace, British Airways, who had a history of seeing off the competition. Remember Freddie Laker?

But, once again, Richard Branson saw opportunity where others saw none, and founded Virgin Atlantic with great success. He proved once again that it is not the facts but what you think about the facts that will determine what happens.

In reality, all of us look for proof that things are actually possible before we try them ourselves. Think back to when you first learned how to drive. Remember how you sat there, with the gear lever with one hand, looking in the mirrors, using your feet to brake, change gear and accelerate all at the same time.

Was it difficult at the beginning? Of course! But as children we all watched adults effortlessly drive their cars, so we knew it was possible and, sure enough, after each lesson it got easier until all those actions became automatic.

No matter how difficult something seems at the beginning as long as we know it is possible, if we are prepared to learn and then practice, everything is possible. In this book I have outlined a number of new skills for you to learn to move your business forward.

To help you to turn these new skills into action I have recorded some video clips in which I show you each step to take. You will be able to pause, rewind and watch them until you are confident about each process.

To view them go to www.4freetips.net

4freetips

Try this free autoresponder and private video uploaded with full telephone support to help you

How to unblock a facebook page, it is important that you watch this one

http://www.youtube.com/watch?v=dO7jWnN_n_Y

How to set up a blog on blogger

http://www.youtube.com/watch?v=zZ-888FkHpQ

How to upload a Youtube video

http://www.youtube.com/watch?v=Slersg8keEg

How to set up facebook fan page

http://www.youtube.com/watch?v=3px0OItPBL0

How to add Twitter to Facebook and your blog

http://www.youtube.com/watch?v=v45QyvC1dhY

How to link to Twitter and facebook with Hootsuite part 1

http://www.youtube.com/watch?v=v45QyvC1dhY

How to link to Twitter and facebook with Hootsuite part 1

http://www.youtube.com/watch?v=h6zQSSCeLP0

How to link to Twitter and facebook with Hootsuite part 2

http://www.youtube.com/watch?v=QsNaamv6J7c

How to add text to you tube video and clickable links

http://www.youtube.com/watch?v=LSu4F23yOBo

How to put words in a picture

http://www.youtube.com/watch?v=ivs_xYOokj8

So, how did we achieve our success?

Many people ask us how did we achieve our success in the business, and more importantly, how could they do the same?

When we started, there was nobody to teach us. We learned by driving miles to meetings, to learn from people who were making it work. We were open minded to learn. We still are today.

Why have we remained open minded?

The following event is clear in my memory. When I was young, working in the shipyard as an engineer, a man in his sixties was talking to me during a tea break. He said he had learned a new skill and was excited about it.

What struck me was that he had been in the shipyards for a lifetime, and yet he was still open to learning something new. I have never forgotten that as it helped me to understand that nobody knows everything.

This has kept me humble and always open to learning new ideas. So stay humble, or you could crumble.

"It is what you learn when
you think you know it all,
that really matters"

Making the numbers work

Whatever business you are in, if you are growing a team and sharing an opportunity with people, you need to accept that you will have to go through the numbers.

When we started in the business, we quickly discovered that there were just three types of people.

- Those that said "Yes"
- Those that said "No"
- And those that said "Maybe"

Of course, those people who said "Yes" are great. However, don't write off the "No"s and the "Maybe"s too quickly. When we first started, we did not realise that when people say "No" what they might actually be saying is "No, I don't know enough to say 'Yes' yet."

The same with the "Maybe", all they need is a bit more evidence. So what we started to do was to post out regular information each month to the "Maybe"s and some of the "No"s. Our mistake was that we did not send it out to everybody.

So, learn from our mistake, and follow up to everyone that doesn't join right away.

Remember, the Fortune is in the Follow up!

Enthusiasm is contagious.
Make sure that yours
is worth catching.

The Power of the Follow Up

We have grown our business to the size it is today by realising the power of following up on everyone, and staying in touch. Especially in these challenging times, people's circumstances can change unexpectedly. You never know when the moment will be right for them to join your business. That is why staying in touch is so important.

The good news is that today technology has made this far easier than it was when we first started. By keeping an open mind, and always being receptive to good ideas, we have developed a whole new range of low-cost and no-cost techniques to do this, which I will now share with you.

At the beginning, we would send out a monthly letter by post. Every time we did that, a few more people would join.

We learned later that you get......

2% of people join on your first contact.

3% on your second contact.

5% on your third contact.

10% on your fourth contact.

80% on your 5th to 12th contact.

Do you see things clearly straight away, or do you need to take a second, or even third look?

OK, so how many triangles do you see?

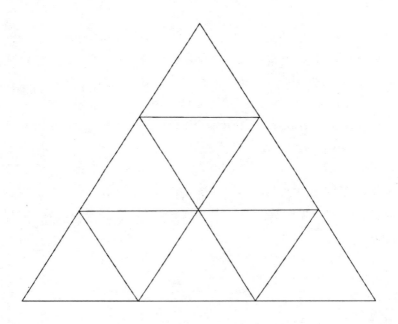

Answer on the next page

Yes, you read that right! Four out of five people joined after five to twelve contacts. What if you could make contact every month or whenever you like, forever?

Well you can. There are now simple and cheap methods of achieving this which I will explain.

Sending out a regular drip feed of information and providing proof that the business works has been one of the reasons that our business has grown to the size it is today. You can do exactly the same.

Some people see things straight away – some do not. Try out these examples for yourself.

Read this sentence just once and count the number of times that the letter "f" appears.

The finished file is the result of years of scientific development and of research.

Answer on the next page — no peeking!

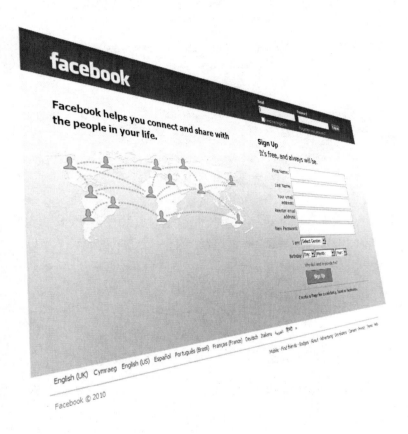

Answers

There are 13 triangles

And six letter "F"s

How many ways are there of staying in touch?

The internet now makes it possible to stay in touch with your prospects without the cost of printing and postage.

These new methods include:

- **Autoresponders**
- **Contact Management systems**
- **Social Networks like Facebook**
- **Twitter**
- **Blogging**
- **YouTube**

Five out of six of those are completely free of charge! Of course, there are many other business and social networks out there, but the principles I will share with you apply to them all.

Don't worry if you've never used any of these systems before. When I first tried them, I was surprised how easy they were to use. I will go into some detail on each of these later in this book, but to help you further, do take a look at the training video clips I have recorded on my website, www.4freetips.net

Email Marketing. Solved.™

Stand out from the crowd!
Send high-impact newsletters, video emails, and follow-up campaigns that hit their revenue targets!

Order Now   Take a Tour

 Create and send beautiful **newsletters** and **followups!**

 Find out what customers want with **FREE online surveys**

 Track customers and analyze campaigns for **higher ROI**

 Grab attention with eye-catching **video emails!**

 Target your business

Beautify your email marketing Choose from 300+ eye-popping newsletter templates!

Featured GetResponse Report

Download

Contact Management Systems

Contact Management Systems are a great way to store email addresses and names. In addition, they offer a facility to create autoresponders which are a great way to leverage your time.

These systems give you the facility to manage your contacts and to keep in touch with them on a regular basis. It does not matter if your list is a few hundred or many thousands, the system can create personalised emails addressed to each person using their first name.

Just think of your own experience. If you looked at your own incoming emails and out of say 25 in your inbox there was one addressed to you by name, which one would you read first? Probably the one with your name in it. The rest you will probably bin!

There are other autoresponders and contact managers that don't insert the first name, but we believe these to be less effective.

A link to the one we use can be found on the website www.4freetips.net and costs under $20 per month and there is even a free option. You will also find training videos on how to use the system. There is also an excellent telephone support system to help you if you get stuck.

Top Features

GetResponse gives you 100s of media-rich email marketing features to create campaigns that convert contacts into customers online, on Twitter, and on target!

Order Now   **Sign Up Free**

Top Features | Features By Category

Form Builder

Create engaging web forms in just a few clicks! Choose from 500+ beautiful templates to pick the perfect design for your business. Customize, resize, drag and drop at will for that "made to measure" look. Add checkboxes, radio buttons and custom fields, then place them wherever you want. Follow up with a dynamic "Thank you page" personalized with audio or video to engage new subscribers right from the start.

Learn more ▸   Watch Video ▸

Email-to-Speech

Email-to-Speech automatically converts text into high-quality human voice so subscribers can listen to your emails "hands free" - no matter where they are or what they're doing! Reach mobile, multi-tasking audiences while they drive, cook dinner, surf the Internet, walk in the park! Email-to-Speech will revolutionize your subscribers' email experience and increase engagement. And that means more revenue for your business!

Learn more ▸   Watch Video ▸

Video Email Marketing

Give a face and a voice to your messages with video email marketing! GetResponse Multimedia Studio lets you record, upload and store up to 1GB of audio and video files, right from your account. Deliver high-impact customer testimonials, product demos, and event videos – no added software or expense required!

Learn more ▸   Watch Video ▸

Advanced Segmentation

Combine behavior and location on the fly for hyper-targeted campaigns. Quickly and easily group your customers based on customer email activity, geography, and profile data collected from web forms and surveys. Choose the perfect mix of criteria to create and send the right messages to the right people at the right time. With GetResponse Advanced Segmentation, you can increase customer engagement, retention and campaign ROI faster than ever before.

Learn more ▸

Social Media Integration

Are your prospects getting their product "buzz" from social networks? If so, you need to be there! GetResponse puts you in the middle of the conversation with powerful integration and social media features that make it easy to share your newsletters across all your networks automatically!

Learn more ▸   Watch Video ▸

iPhone Application

Keep your finger on the pulse of your campaigns! GetResponse iPhone App gives you instant access to your dashboard and key stats, so you can react, anywhere, anytime. Add subscribers manually or import from your Address Book and you'll never miss an opportunity to grow your list.

free Get started for Free!

Login:

Password:

Confirm password:

First name:

Email:

Sign Up Free

We are here to help!

Contact Us

☎ Call 1-877-EMAIL-GR

✉ Send Email

💬 Live Chat

How to use an Autoresponder

We have a saying - "facts tell, stories sell", which has worked for years in our business and will work in any situation. Use stories whenever you can - they work!

Here is another tip;

If you have not caught their attention in the first two lines, your e-mail is toast. They will delete it. Make sure that you start your email in an interesting way. The question that they will be asking is "What's in it for me?"

But, before we give you some tips on what to put in e-mails, first you must make sure that your web page obtains their name, address, phone number and most importantly an e-mail address. Without this you are wasting your time.

This is done using a squeeze page (also called a grab page or a capture form). So ensure your website has such a page.

The trick to get people to put in details is to offer something for free. This is often described as a "Golden Carrot". In your case, what you are offering is information on how they can earn a second income, or get out of debt.

Here is a list of magic words/phrases

Free
Fill in your details for free DVD

Announcing new offer
Fill in your details for free DVD

Introducing/special offer.
Fill in your details for free info

New/best offer yet.
Fill in your details for free DVD

Secrets/we reveal them
Fill in your details for free info

How to/find out now
Fill in your details

Guarantee/see how it works free
Fill in your details

Magic/find why
Fill in your details

Easy/free help
Fill in your details

Your website can have a big button or a drop down flag to catch their details, using one of the headers above.

You can test different ones to see which works best for you. Many businesses use this system to great effect.

Generating a response

For your Lead Generating website to work, you need to know as much about your potential customer as possible.

What is it they are looking for? How will what you are offering make a difference to them?

It doesn't matter what business you are in, there are seven reasons that people will buy.

Seven Reasons People Buy

1. They know you, like you and trust you
2. They need to make money
3. They want to save money
4. They want to save time
5. They want to save effort - make it easy
6. Improve their health or lifestyle
7. Eliminate pain or discomfort

If your website targets one or more of these top seven reasons that people buy, then you are on the right track. Choose a good headline that will catch their attention and make sure that what you are offering them, your free report, your brochure or your "Golden Carrot" provides them with the answer to their needs.

"I don't have any yet. We just opened."

Choosing your domain name

One of the most important things when choosing a domain name is to make it short, easy to remember and relevant to the subject.

Take a tip from one of the most successful websites, worldwide - the BBC. Not surprisingly they didn't rush out to register
www.thebritishbroadcastingcompany.co.uk
Why? Because it takes too long to type in, and is far too long. Instead they sensibly opted for www.bbc.co.uk

Remember the acronym K.I.S.S - Keep It Simple, Stupid. Your website address should be easy to remember and have no slashes. Try remembering
www.bbc.co.uk/sport/hi-football/default.stm
Trips off the tongue doesn't it?

Sometimes using dashes can make a phrase easier to read and also easier for the search engines to work with. It can also help you to find a domain name which otherwise might have been taken. For example, www.make-me-rich-now.com was still available at the time of going to press.

Try to find a word or phrase that relates to the need that people have or the problem they are trying to solve.

Enthusiasm and the power of personal recommendations are the foundations of every successful business

Building a relationship

One of the great advantages of using an autoresponder system, and using it to communicate with people on a regular basis, is that it enables you to build rapport and, over time, a relationship with them.

Through the content of your emails they will get to know you, and hopefully get to like you and trust you. The three ingredients necessary if they are to consider joining your business.

My advice would be, don't just rush in for the kill. Play it steadily. Share stories, share good news, share achievements. Be positive and demonstrate that you care.

How do you feel when you walk into a shop and an assistant rushes across to you and asks you what you want to buy? Whoa! Slow down. Let me browse first! It should be the same with your emails. Let them browse.

Of course, you have two other powerful tools at your disposal. Your own enthusiasm and the power of personal recommendation. These are the two pillars on which this industry is built. Use them to your advantage in your regular emails.

It is news that sells newspapers.
Make your message immediate,
topical, relevant and exciting.
The first thing people want to
know is, "What's in it for me?"

Now let us suppose that you are in that same shop and instead of an assistant rushing across to you and putting you under pressure, you bump into one of your friends who greets you warmly by name.

It just happens that your friend is knowledgeable on the products you are interested in buying, and shares with you their experience and their personal recommendation. Because of the trust and the relationship you have with your friend, you now go ahead and purchase the item.

Always remember this when you are communicating with your prospects. Once they know you, like you and trust you, they will be receptive to your personal recommendation and join your business.

Have you ever been at a special promotion or an open day at a store or a garage, where they sent you an invitation to join them and enjoy free snacks or maybe cheese and wine? The refreshments were just a carrot to get you into their showroom. You can use that same technique to build your list and fill your sales funnel with prospects.

Offer a "Golden Carrot" of something that will be useful to them, and that is free, in return for their contact details, so you can add them to your list and start building that all important relationship.

Water may be soft to the touch, gentle and healthy,
but it can have other properties as well.

If you allow a drop of water to fall a few feet
in the same place, time and time again,
it will eventually make a hole -
even in granite, the hardest of all rocks.

Regular communication can breakdown
resistance, and produce the desired result.

But only if you are persistent!

Make it interesting!

One of the things I have learned over the years is to make my regular emails different and interesting.

However, you may have noticed that I also keep them very simple and text based with lots of web links.

If you start to be clever with graphics and images, you may find that your emails sometimes don't get through as they have been stopped by the spam filters. This is another reason to K.I.S.S - Keep it Simple, Stupid!

The other reason for keeping it simple is that it is quick to do. If you start to spend long hours trying to polish the look and design of your autoresponders, you are stealing time from yourself that could be far more productively used. Take a tip from me, I know the results I get from my emails, and they could not be simpler. Don't try to reinvent the wheel!

However, in addition to the many stories and tips which I give away, I do make some of my message video clips or pictures. It is no bad thing to add some variety into the way you regularly communicate. But you will notice that I just put a link in the message to the clip rather than building it into the message itself, which would be a lot more complicated.

Think excitement,
talk excitement,
act out excitement,
and you are bound to
become an exciting person.
Life will take on a new zest,
deeper interest,
and greater meaning.

Norman Vincent Peale

Stay Positive

We live in a negative world. Newspapers are full of bad news, so is the television. Any message that is upbeat and positive will always stand out and get attention.

Be careful not to use negative words in your messages as it won't encourage people to respond. Also, you need to positively position yourself as someone with something worth finding out more about, and as someone you would want to meet. If you come across as negative, people will cross the street when they see you coming!

Let your enthusiasm shine through in everything you write. You have a business that you are proud of. You are achieving positive results. You are helping others to discover they can do things they had never thought of before, and they are becoming successful as a result.

Share all those positives. Make your writing interesting, current and relevant. Never over hype, it always comes over as false and unbelievable. Just use real stories about real people who are moving towards their goals step by step. And always avoid any mention of religion, sport or politics - keep it neutral and free of offence.

Finally, always leave people wanting to know more. Make them curious and wanting to know more - just like the end of a soap on television.

facebook

Facebook helps you connect and share with the people in your life.

Email

☐ Keep me logged in

Sign Up
It's free, and

First Name:

Last Name

Your em
addre

Reenter e
add

New Pass

English (UK)   Cymraeg   English (US)   Español   Português (Brasil)   Français (France)   Deutsch   Italiano   العربية   हिन्दी

Mobile · Find fri

Facebook © 2010

Using Facebook

At the time of writing, Facebook had 500 million people on it. However, it is growing at such a speed that one billion (1000 million) people are soon going to be on it.

What started as a mega site for young people to connect with each other is turning into a massive business tool. If Facebook get it right, and they are currently working into building a search tool, they may overtake Google.

So if you thought Facebook was just for kids to play games on and to put silly pictures up, think again! It's fast becoming a marketing tool for people who understand how to use it correctly. As you probably know, Facebook is free and you have very little control over the way a normal Facebook site is constructed.

In fact, if you try and run a business through a normal Facebook site you may well be shut down. It happened to us! At that time we had 3,000 friends on our site, but they still shut us down. No matter how much begging we did they would not put it back. In fact, you cannot pick the phone up to them and even e-mails are just standard replies.

However, there is a way round it. So learn from our mistakes.

You can set up a Facebook fan page. The pop stars have had them for a while and because people have clicked to join the group, there are different rules to your advantage.

I've done a video on our training website to show you how to set up a fan page on www.4freetips.net

Every social networking site has its own set of rules, but they don't always make them obvious. As a result , it can be very easy to get shut down.

Obviously it makes sense that you are not rude and do not send negative e-mails to people. If you are foolish enough to do so, they can complain and get your site shut down.

Here are some things you need to be aware of to stop your account getting shut down.

When you first register on Facebook, there is a option you can select that informs all your e-mail contacts that you are a member of Facebook. Your real friends will receive this, click on the link, and add you as a friend on their Facebook page.

Now, as you use Facebook yourself, you will get excited and start clicking on different pictures to invite other people to become your friend as well. But be warned.

This is the first way you can get your Facebook site shut down. You see, once you have asked a set number of people to join you and they don't, you are seen as a spammer.

There are also automatic programmes which you can use to add people as Facebook friends in bulk. Not surprisingly, Facebook is wise to these systems and is quick to identify it as spam. Be warned!

If you send business messages to a normal Facebook page, again Facebook spot it and your account may shut down.

If you decide to run a advert from your normal Facebook page, it will spot that as well. Once you set up a fan Facebook page and use that to send an advert it will also get turned down. Facebook is very clever at spotting something fishy. Get caught a couple of times, and you are shut down.

If you were to set an advert up and then change the website without notifying them, again you will be shut down again.

To avoid many of the above issues, set up a Facebook fan page. I have recorded a video to show you exactly how to do this. You can watch it on www.4freetips.net

What you can do is to add a link on your Facebook page to invite people to join your fan page. You can also have a button on your website, your blog, on YouTube and also on Twitter to increase your fan base.

The exciting thing about a Facebook fan page is that you can reach your entire list of fans with one e-mail.

Now, using this very powerful tool, you can send a message to a few hundred people or to literally millions of people, if you want to go big time.

All messages posted on the Facebook fan page are indexed by Google and there is a site called Hootsuite where you can add all your updates to Twitter, YouTube, and blog at the same time.

With a Facebook fan page, you can use pictures and stories and videos as well. This gives you the option to go viral. It's good to ask for comments. If you have a few hundred fans and a person leaves a comment, all their friends will see it. The compound effect of this is massive.

Once again, I have prepared a video to explain this on www.4freetips.net

So make sure your profile picture is positive, happy and totally focused on what you do.

How do you picture yourself?

If your profile picture is a cat, it might mean a lot to you but nothing to anyone else.

Remember, you only ever get one chance to make a first impression. So choose a good photo of yourself and upload it. Make sure you look at your best and happy! Who would want to make contact with somebody looking miserable?

Make sure your profile page has links to twitter, your blog, your YouTube account and your website.

Twitter

Twitter is growing at mega speed... We have a twitter account that links updates on our Facebook page and to our blog.

Twitter accepts only very short messages, so if you share a really long weblink or YouTube link with a long code or blog code, it needs to be shortened.

To shorten it, copy and paste it into this site:

http://bit.ly/

It will shorten to a small link. Now the clever thing is you can track through the above site to see how many people have clicked on your link.

Again make sure your twitter page has a good picture. By posting regular updates, people will find your site and become your followers.

Regular posts to Twitter linked to your blog and Facebook fan page builds your followers and contact list. More videos to link everything are on our training website.

www.4freetips.net

Definition

A blog (a blend of the term web log) is a type of website or part of a website. Blogs are usually maintained by an individual with regular entries of commentary, descriptions of events, or other material such as graphics or video. Entries are commonly displayed in reverse-chronological order.

Most blogs are interactive, allowing visitors to leave comments and even message each other via widgets on the blogs and it is this interactivity that distinguishes them from other static websites

Blogs

We have two blogger sites and a Wordpress site.

Let's look at Blogger first.

Blogger is run by Google which is great to get you out there on the net and index your blogs. There is a video on our support website all about how to set it up.

Take a look at www.4freetips.net

Once you have set your blog up, you can link Facebook fan page, Twitter updates and your website to it. People will start to follow your blog too.

This might seem a lot of work, but it's the same information being shared and all are linked together and might only take a few minutes to upload to all sites. With Blogger it links to Google e-mail which owns YouTube and the same password works on all those sites.

Make sure you have a good picture and background and a good name for your blog.

68 Categories
131 Tags

O Pending
26 Spam

Theme Twenty Ten with 3 Widgets
You are using **WordPress 3.0**.

Change Theme

WordPress is web software you can use to create a beautiful website or blog. We like to say that WordPress is both free and priceless at the same time.

QuickPress

Title

Upload/Insert

Content

The core software is built by hundreds of community volunteers, and when you're ready for more there are thousands of plugins and themes available to transform your site into almost anything you can imagine. Over 25 million people have chosen WordPress to power the place on the web they call "home" — we'd love you to join the family.

Ready to get started? **Download WordPress 3.0.3**

WordPress Books

WordPress MU 2.7
Beginner's Guide

News From Our Blog

WordPress 3.1 Beta 2
Haikus from Jane on her 39th birthday:
Practice makes perfect is what they say about things, but sometimes it's not. In this case it is not practice but refinement, and then more testing. You can help WordPress! Now: 3.1, beta 2 is here; needs testing. But! Remember this: Only install on test sites, as YMMV...

It's Easy As...

1. Find a Web Host and get great hosting while supporting WordPress at the same time.

2. Download & Install WordPress with our famous 5-minute installation. Feel like a rock star.

3. Read the Documentation and become a WordPress expert yourself, impress your friends.

WordPress Users

... and hundreds more

CODE IS POETRY

Privacy : License / GPL   See also: WordPress.com : WordPress.TV : WordCamp : WP Jobs : Matt : Blog RSS

Like   163805 likes. Sign Up to see what your friends like.

Wordpress

Wordpress is yet another way to blog, and it gives you a different way for people to find you on the net.

Wordpress is an open source project and is growing all the time as people contribute additional facilities to it. You don't need to be technical to use it and it is completely customisable. It is very much in your interests to feed as much material as you can onto the internet and this is a great way to do it.

Simply copy and paste the same information from Blogger onto Wordpress. Make sure your Wordpress blog is linked to your Twitter feed and also to your Facebook fan page. Your Wordpress will also have its own subscriber list.

It is very simple to set up and I have recorded a video to take you though every stage. Once again go to www.4freetips.net and click on the Wordpress link

On both Wordpress and Blogger, there are buttons to take you to your visitor statistics so you can monitor the effects of what you do. These days it is not enough to have just one blog. We have learnt that you need to use every possible opportunity to get your message out there.

Search | Browse | TV Shows | Upload

Follow Megan Fox on...

Join the largest worldwide video-sharing community!

Create Account › Already have an account? Sign In

Spo
Pr
P
c
c

Catch Up on the Latest TV

Create a "Perfect Christmas" with Kirstie and Phil, follow two men involved with Al Quaeda in "I Was Bin Laden's Bodyguard", review a creative life in "Any Human Heart" and forget the current cold with "Beach Volleyball" from Huntington Beach, California.

Kirstie and Phil's
from Kirstie and Phil...
More than a week ago

I Was Bin Laden's
from I Was Bin Laden's...
More than a week ago

Any Human Heart - Any
from Any Human Heart
More than a week ago

Beach Volleyball - AVP
from Beach Volleyball
More than a week ago

Recommended for You   Learn More

Edit

Personalised video recommendations
Getting personalised recommendations is really easy, all you have to do is watch some videos, then come back to this page to see what videos YouTube has recommended just for you!

Most Popular

Entertainment

FAMILY GUY - "All I
Really Want ...
210,052 viewis

Music

Cheryl Cole Th
on the Royal V
27,004 views

Right now, You Tube is the most powerful way of getting your message out, for two good reasons.

Firstly, if a picture paints a thousand words, what does a video do?

Secondly, You Tube can be very viral. Sometimes millions of views within a couple of days. Remember the Susan Boyle X Factor YouTube clip?

It's free to set up and it's easy. If you don't know how, we have done a video on our support site to show you. www.4freetips.net

Just like all of the other tools I have been sharing with you, with YouTube you don't have to be a pro to do it.

Neither does your video have to be TV or movie quality. It is the content and the words that count.

One of our first videos had 1000 views a week. Where else could you achieve this exposure for no cost? Indeed if you were doing a Google Keywords campaign to reach your customers, how much would you expect to have to pay to achieve those results?

As a way of demonstrating how easy it is to attract interest on YouTube, I created a short video on Moles. A problem that many people have in their gardens. If you put "how to kill moles" into the YouTube search window, you will find that comes out on top. If you put the same words into Google search it is on the front page.

There is nothing about the video that is cruel but it does show you how to move moles off your land. Now we are not mole catchers, but we do know how to put a video up. Check it out and you'll see what I mean.

Another video we produced for YouTube is called "party plan training". Put that into the YouTube search window, and also into Google, you will see it is on the front page, before millions of other results. That is how well the system works

Once you have your YouTube account, make sure you link it to your Facebook page and your Twitter feed and blog.

Just like Facebook, people can ask to be your friend and your subscriber on YouTube. This gives you the power to share a video with all your friends and your subscribers in one go.

The maximum length for a YouTube video is ten minutes. However, you can get around this by making the programme in sections and having a follow on video. You can also add a link to another video..

Don't miss the opportunity of adding further information in the Comments box. This can create a never ending source of traffic.

Once again, as with your other social networking tools, cross reference them by adding links to your Facebook fan page, your blog and also Twitter. The magic is in using them all and cross promoting each one

You can add these links straightaway, or change them once the video is posted.

Watch my YouTube training video on my site, www.4freetips.net

There is no limit to how many videos you can put up on YouTube.

Once you have activated your site, you can add bubbles to point people to join your Facebook fan page, Twitter or blog and at the top to subscribe to your video.

Displayed above the video when you are logged in, you can see who has been viewing your video, what age, what county, and what key words they searched on to find it. This will be a great help with your future marketing.

Do make sure that you back up all your video clips in another location to YouTube. If your YouTube account got shut down all of that material would be lost.

The autoresponder site I covered earlier also has a facility to let you back up your video there in a private area.

Once again, I urge you to watch the detailed training videos I have created to help you with all of this. I take you through each stage, step by step, on the site itself. Go to www.4freetips.net

Keeping your eggs in one basket

All of the social networking sites and the tools which I have been covering in this book are free and a great way to build a massive list of contacts.

However, a word of warning. Because they are free you do not have much control over them, and it might be that, for no good reason, or as a result of a simple mistake, you might find yourself shut out of your account, or it closed altogether without warning.

My advice is not to rely on just one system. Use them all. Back up everything you can so that, if the site does lock you out, you have not lost any of your lists or material.

However, the biggest tip I could give you is to store all your contacts on your autoresponder or contact manager. That way they will be safe, after all you are paying for the service. If you did lose your Facebook account you could then just e-mail everybody and inform them of your new account.

I have also produced training videos on this subject on the training video site.

Of course, it goes without saying that you should also cover every eventuality by backing up your lists on your PC every now and again.

Your list, and indeed all your other data is very precious, and the success of your business depends on it being kept safe.

Many home computers are used by more than one person, and it is very easy for mistakes to be made, and for things to be deleted by accident. No hard drive ever made will last for ever, and what with the constant attacks by viruses, we all need to be very aware of the value of the information we are storing.

There are many ways to keep it safe. We once had an external hard drive but it died, and we lost all our information.

As a result, what we use now is a site called 'Squirrel Save'. It currently costs £4.99 per month and it backs up everything automatically, storing it on a remote secure servers which are themselves backed up. It certainly gives us peace of mind.

As far as all your social networks and communication tools are concerned, the one thing we have learnt is to make sure that everything links to each other.

That way you reach the maximum of people and, by communicating regularly, that little "drip, drip" of information may well bring them into your business. .

Together, your autoresponder, your accounts on Twitter, and Facebook, your blogs, and your YouTube videos, create an incredibly a powerful marking tool.

Remember, it was water which opened up and created the Grand Canyon. Certainly it took probably millions of years, but it was the drip, drip of water which created it. You can use that same "drip, drip" of information to make your message memorable.

There is an old saying that you have to tell somebody something seven times before they remember.

Just think the last time you met somebody new and they said their name. Five minutes later you had forgotten it. What is more, they had probably forgotten yours as well!

If it takes hearing something seven times before we remember it when it's simple - what if it's not simple? What if it's complicated? What if it requires some kind of significant adjustment in someone's personal or business life? What chance is there that they will "get it" first time, and then remember it?

You see most people hate change. The more difficult it is, the harder it will be to learn, or for it to sink in. That is why we were taught to recite the "timestables" at school over and over again, so that we would remember it. Repetition works.

You can never tell when the time will be right for somebody to suddenly wake up to your opportunity, even if you have been in contact with them regularly for some time. Sometimes it takes a life changing event, like redundancy, to focus their mind. Then they see it. Nobody can predict when the time is right. That is why you need to stay in contact.

Most people overestimate what they can do in one year and they greatly underestimate what they can do in five years. But by using all the systems and tools I have included in this book, things will definitely move faster for you then ever before.

So start building your list to make your own "Grand Canyon" of a business to take you to your goals. Make the power of numbers really work for you.

Finally, keep going back to www.4freetips.net, as I will be adding new videos there regularly.

Leaders are Readers

As I said earlier in the book, it is stories that are one of the most powerful tools in building your business. Your stories and also other people's stories.

In building our business over the years I have used one book to great effect. It is

The 45 Second Presentation by Don Fallia

When I originally read this book I could not sleep with excitement. When people you talk to say they know everything about MLM, I just say have you read this book? If they say no, they know nothing about MLM. I have sponsored so many people over the years by just letting them read this book.

You see I was so bad at school at reading that I knew a book had to capture your attention fast. These books are very simple to read and get you excited.

95% of the population are not highly educated and we need that percentage of the population to build a business in MLM.

The 5% who are highly educated and can read the books quickly, may be on a good income, but not used to the income and lifestyle that can be earned in MLM. So use the books, they work! Make sure your team has access to more training and personal development books.

I have read loads over the years, a lot of the books are on tape or CD. This gives you a great opportunity to learn while you drive and with traffic so bad now, you might as well be learning in your car.

When you were at school you were told to learn your timetables off by heart. Listen to the tapes ten times and you will pick up all the information. As you are driving you have to concentrate on the driving at some point and miss a bit on tape or CD. So listen again and again.

Some other books to read:-

- Big Al Books
- Skill With People
- Rhino Success
- How to Win Friends and Influence People
- Think and Grow Rich
- MLM Nuts and Bolts

Using Voice Messaging

One of the tools that has made the biggest impact on our business over the years has been the use of a Voice Messaging System.

Voice Messaging is a great way to leverage your time. You can communicate with all your team with just one phone call, and they can pick up your message at a time that is convenient to them. Your teams can also use the system to communicate with each other, to share stories, good news, training , news of events and company information. It is a very powerful tool.

Interestingly, some research was done in the USA by author Edward Ludbrook. Two network marketing groups were independently monitored for a year. One group used voice messaging. The other did not.

The results were staggering.

	Messaging group	Non-messaging group
Renewed contracts	90%	30%
New people recruited others	40%	10%
Stayed active	92%	46%
Regular contact with sponsor	97%	57%

You can see from the chart that the group who used voice messaging turned over 100% more products than the group that didn't.

This research was done over one year, but if you extrapolate the results over five years, the group using voice messaging grows by 350% and is as strong as any I have been associated with over the years.

The other group slowly declines and ends up as just one - you!

These results speak for themselves. However, it is not enough to just be on the voice mail system. You also have to use it well. Here are some hints and tips to help you to do just that.

Voice Messaging Hints and Tips

A voice messaging system should be run by one leader. This person should be in charge of putting out a daily positive message. From my experience, the maximum length of any message should only be a couple of minutes and it works. Best if it goes out at the same time every day. People like predictability.

This lets the team know that a leader is setting a good positive example. I have been putting out a message at 9:00am every morning for 7 years.

If I am on holiday in a different time zone I put the message out so that it arrives at 9:00am UK time, so there is a positive message in the morning when the team gets up.

Your group messages should be a mixture of stories about Retail, Products, Sponsoring and Lifestyle. Most good messaging companies will also have also have industry experts leaving a message at least once a week.

A good messaging system will allow you to link a story to your message. In the early months I used to just tell a story I had heard. However, people thought I was making it up. If you hear other people telling their own story in their own words, it has more credibility and gives belief.

Look out for positive stories that support the business in newspapers, magazine or on television. Spread the word on the system so people can get copies of their own to share with their teams or their prospects.

Remember the saying - "Facts Tell, Stories Sell"

Finally, I do hope you have found the information I have shared with you in this to be helpful. But knowledge on its own will not make you rich.

If it did, every academic would be driving a Porsche, rather than a bicycle. It is not what you know, but what you do that counts.

Put what you've learnt into action, and keep your mind always open to learning something new, and you too will end up enjoying the success you truly deserve.

Gavin

It is easier to get rich than to make excuses

Jim Rohn